CONTENTS

I0799671

BOLDFACE WORDS APPEAR IN THE GLOSSARY.

THE LIBERATOR

Abraham Lincoln was the 16th president of the United States. Many people believe he was the greatest president. Abraham was a skilled speaker and strong leader. His actions helped **liberate** African Americans from **slavery**.

DISCOVER!

PEOPLE of the PAST

WHO WAS ABRAHAM LINCOLN?

Robert Clore

Enslow PUBLISHING

Please visit our website, www.enslow.com. For a free color catalog of all our high-quality books, call toll free 1-800-398-2504 or fax 1-877-980-4454.

Cataloging-in-Publication Data
Names: Clore, Robert.
Title: Who was Abraham Lincoln? / Robert Clore.
Description: Buffalo, NY : Enslow Publishing, 2027. | Series: People of the past | Includes glossary.
Identifiers: ISBN 9781978550445 (pbk.) | ISBN 9781978550452 (library bound) | ISBN 9781978550469 (ebook)
Subjects: LCSH: Lincoln, Abraham, 1809-1865–Juvenile literature. | Presidents–United States–Biography–Juvenile literature. | Legislators–United States–Biography–Juvenile literature.
Classification: LCC E457.905 C657 2027 | DDC 973.7092 B–dc23

Published in 2027 by
Enslow Publishing
2544 Clinton Street
Buffalo, NY 14224

Copyright © 2027 Enslow Publishing

Designer: Claire Vanden Branden
Editor: Max Pritchard

Photo Credits: Cover, pp. 1, 15 Everett Collection/Shutterstock.com; p. 5 Alexander Gardner/Library of Congress; p. 7 Internet Archive; pp. 9, 11, 13, 17 Library of Congress; p. 19 National Archives; p. 21 Sergii Figurnyi/Shutterstock.com.

All rights reserved. No part of this book may be reproduced in any form without permission in writing from the publisher, except by a reviewer.

Printed in China

CPSIA compliance information: Batch #QS27ENS: For further information contact Enslow Publishing, at 1-800-398-2504.

Find us on

EARLY LIFE

Abraham was born in Kentucky on February 12, 1809. His family moved to Indiana in 1816 and to Illinois in 1830. Abraham didn't go to school but learned to read and write. After working many different jobs, he studied law and became a successful lawyer.

ABRAHAM WORKING
AS A RAIL SPLITTER

In 1842, Abraham married Mary Todd. They had four sons. Edward and William died very young. The others were named Robert and Thomas. Robert was the only son to live to adulthood. He became a successful lawyer and businessman.

ENTERING POLITICS

Abraham was **elected** to the US **House of Representatives** in 1847. He ran against his rival, Stephen A. Douglas, for US **Senate** in 1858. The two men took part in popular political **debates**. Abraham lost the Senate election, but many people thought he was a talented speaker.

STEPHEN A. DOUGLAS

PRESIDENTIAL ELECTION

Abraham was elected US president in 1860. After his election, South Carolina **seceded** from the United States. Ten more states followed. They were worried that Abraham would outlaw slavery. These states formed the Confederate States of America.

AN 1860 PORTRAIT OF ABRAHAM LINCOLN

CIVIL WAR

Abraham wanted to keep the United States together. He was willing to go to war to do this. The American **Civil War** began in 1861. As the war continued, Abraham began working to stop slavery. Meanwhile, he supported settlement of the west, threatening the livelihoods of Native Americans.

ABRAHAM MEETS WITH SOME OF HIS GENERALS.

On January 1, 1863, Abraham issued the Emancipation Proclamation. The order said that all enslaved people living in Confederate states were free. Soon after, Abraham gave a famous speech known as the Gettysburg Address. He honored those who had died during the Civil War.

THE GETTYSBURG ADDRESS

ABRAHAM'S SECOND TERM

In 1864, Abraham was elected president again. He helped push the Thirteenth Amendment through Congress. This changed the **US Constitution** to outlaw slavery in 1865. He met with Confederate leaders to end the war. He did not succeed at first, but on April 9, 1865, the Confederate leaders surrendered.

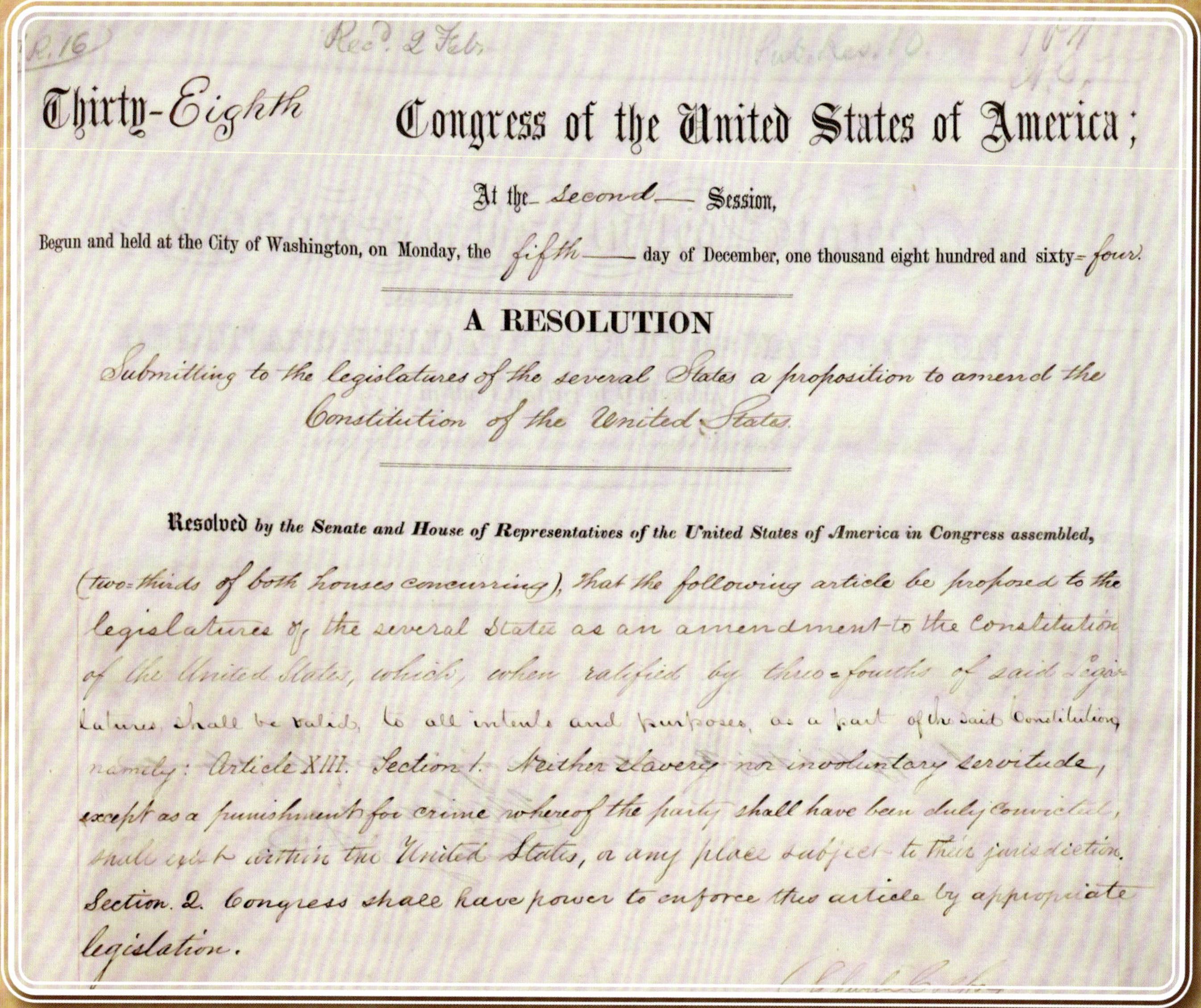
R. 16 Rec^d. 2 Feb. Pub. Res. 10.

Thirty-Eighth Congress of the United States of America;

At the Second Session,

Begun and held at the City of Washington, on Monday, the fifth day of December, one thousand eight hundred and sixty-four.

A RESOLUTION

Submitting to the legislatures of the several States a proposition to amend the Constitution of the United States.

Resolved by the Senate and House of Representatives of the United States of America in Congress assembled, (two-thirds of both houses concurring), that the following article be proposed to the legislatures of the several States as an amendment to the Constitution of the United States, which, when ratified by three-fourths of said Legislatures shall be valid, to all intents and purposes, as a part of the said Constitution, namely: Article XIII. Section 1. Neither slavery nor involuntary servitude, except as a punishment for crime whereof the party shall have been duly convicted, shall exist within the United States, or any place subject to their jurisdiction. Section 2. Congress shall have power to enforce this article by appropriate legislation.

THE THIRTEENTH AMENDMENT

ASSASSINATION

John Wilkes Booth shot Abraham in Ford's Theatre on April 14, 1865. Abraham died on April 15. Abraham's leadership had brought the country back together. He will continue to stand as one of the most important figures in US history.

THE LINCOLN MEMORIAL
IN WASHINGTON, DC

GLOSSARY

civil war: A war between two groups within a country.

debates: Discussions between people with different ideas about an issue.

elected: Chosen for a position in a government.

House of Representatives: One part of the US Congress, which makes laws.

liberate: To free someone being controlled by another person or group.

seceded: For part of a country to have broken away and formed its own country.

Senate: The upper chamber of the US Congress, which makes laws.

slavery: The state of being owned by another person and forced to work without pay.

US Constitution: The piece of writing stating the rules of the United States government.

FOR MORE INFORMATION

Books

Fontes, Justine. *Abraham Lincoln*. New York, NY: DK Publishing, 2025.

Rumsch, BreAnn. *Abraham Lincoln*. North Mankato, MN: Abdo, 2025.

Stanchak, John. *Civil War*. New York, NY: DK Publishing, 2023.

Websites

Britannica Kids: Abraham Lincoln
kids.britannica.com/kids/article/Abraham-Lincoln/345491
Read about Abraham Lincoln's life and find related articles.

National Geographic Kids: Celebrating Juneteenth
kids.nationalgeographic.com/history/article/celebrating-juneteenth
Juneteenth celebrates the freedom of enslaved people.

Publisher's note to educators and parents: Our editors have carefully reviewed these websites to ensure that they are suitable for students. Many websites change frequently, however, and we cannot guarantee that a site's future contents will continue to meet our high standards of quality and educational value. Be advised that students should be closely supervised whenever they access the internet.

INDEX